SOAK

An Homage to Water

Wren Farris

Printed in the United States by IngramSpark

Edited by: Katie Vecchio | www.katievecchio.com

Book Cover and Author Photos by: Jes Klien Photography | www.jesklein.com

Book Cover and Author Photo Detail Work: Mark Sandvig | www.bellafotophotography.com

Book Cover and Interior design by: Vanessa Mendozzi | www.vanessamendozzidesign.com

Feather image used under license "Shutterstock.com"

Bird track image by Wren Farris

Library of Congress Control Number:

Farris, Wren

Soak: An Homage to Water

ISBN: 978-0-9978891-0-9

Contents

Names and other intimate details have been intentionally modified to preserve privacy.

"Pure water is the world's first and foremost medicine."
—Slovakian Proverb

Introduction
WATER. AN HOMAGE

{1}

Between the ages of twenty-seven and thirty I was hit twice by drunk drivers on rural New Mexico roads. The similarities between the two car accidents were haunting—wintertime, a big black truck, hit and run, almost three years apart to the day—and in both accidents, in a tandem echo that still haunts me to this day, the first officer to arrive on the scene walked straight over and said, "There is no way you should be alive."

After these experiences, the conventional Western medical system had no real answers for putting me back together. My body, mind, and psyche had become hot, agitated, restless, angry, and tormented. Thus began a journey of mythic proportions and magical encounters, a sinuous ten-year road of alternative healing modalities, shamanic practices, and vision quests that led directly to Water. Lakes, rivers, oceans, hot springs, hot tubs, waterfalls, streams, a bowl of water placed in the moonlight, rivulets of rain on a window, tears, icebergs, glaciers, bathtubs, all forms of rain...Unlike the fire inside, everything water was cool, blue, calm, healing, ease.

Eventually, all the water I could find in New Mexico just wasn't enough. I moved to the sea and frequented every form of flowing water I could get myself into or near. I began to orient my days around the next chance to be in water—the river, the hot springs, the bathtub. Things changed. The red in my mind started to turn blue. My body untangled as I gave it the gift of the weightless remembering of being pain-free that occurred for me in water.

And then this happened...

I kept hearing about a small artsy town on the tip of a peninsula surrounded by water. By the third time that someone said, "You would *love* it there! It's exactly your kind of place!" I got in the car and went to find out what they meant. It had been seven years since my first car accident.

The evening I arrived, I walked the cool rainy downtown streets looking in shop windows filled with Pendleton blankets and Native American art, and was greeted by friendly dog-walking Northwesterners. Soaking up the town's stunning backdrop of omnipresent water, I asked around to find out if there was a bathhouse or some hot springs nearby where I could warm my bones. Nothing.

Dusk happened quickly and the wind was cold. I stepped into a pub, sat down, got out my journal, and out of nowhere downloaded from my mind an entire plan to build a bathhouse in this little town that I had never been to before. It was like a premonition. I even wrote down the financials, the detailed business structure, and physical layout of the space.

To be clear, I had *no* intention of moving to this town—or of starting a business! I was working on a half-built house in New Mexico, was wracked with chronic pain, and had just split up with my fiancé. At that moment, I had no work and no foreseeable path. The writing exercise was nothing but a daydream. I left the bar and walked back down Water Street under a hard rain, feeling lonely and lost in a town at the end of nowhere, knowing no one.

In the light of morning, as I walked the beach accompanied only by the echo of the foghorn, something sublime washed over me—again like a premonition. I glimpsed that I had arrived at a final section of road, however long still, that led to the end of my pain. Something deep inside me spoke: *The beauty here—the water—will put you back together.*

I moved to the sweet little town, rented a studio apartment, and spent most of my time at the water's edge, grieving, healing, and swimming in the cold waters of the Puget Sound. I was virtually pain-free within a month and, as my psyche had some space to breathe again, I realized I was emerging from my long-endured underworld journey with an unforeseen gift: I had healed from what doctors had called unhealable. I had survived (twice!) a situation that others do not. And I wanted to give a gift back to the world in a tangible way.

Three years later, Soak on the Sound was born in this place. A first-of-its-kind salt-water bathhouse, 'Soak' is a sanctuary where people participate in their own wellness and transformations. It is *surprisingly* close to what came through in the unpremeditated free-write at the bar that first night I wearily came to town.

And I owe it all to the water...

{2}

In the tenuous inaugural months when Soak on the Sound's doors first opened, some of the locals were skeptical of the concept of a bathhouse. "How are things going?" they would ask. "I mean, how are you going to *make* it?"

I knew exactly what they meant. *It's too fringe. Isn't it 'weird' to undress in public? Is it clean? We just don't do that in our culture...*

And I remember the first time I uttered a reply that rippled through me with absolute knowing. "You just can't keep people away from water," I said.

{3}

The nine vignettes in this book span a ten-year healing journey guided by being in, near, and around water and are snapshots of what occurred on the path that led to birthing the vision we call Soak. The landscapes straddle between the hot spring laden Southwest desert and the wet and luscious seascapes of the Pacific Northwest. These essays do not follow a clear thru-line, except water, as the healing itself had no clear trajectory. I followed it day-by-day, era-by-era, wherever it led, whatever was required, often becoming more undone on the path to being put back together.

Part I
{Undress}

Chapter 1

THE SIMPLE SENSUOUS DELIGHT OF BEING WET

{1}

In one era of my New Mexico years I bought a dilapidated, half-built, off-the-grid straw-bale house on a remote and rugged mesa with hundred-mile views, searing sun, and an almost ceaseless wind. The water that flowed into the house came from a rainwater catchment system that captured and stored any rain and snow that fell throughout the year. Monitoring the water level and health of the cisterns was a daily affair. Monsoon season and winter snows were especially joyful times, as was any passing squall that delivered rain. I learned rain-dances and water prayers, and, at times, those charms were direly needed. During winter freezes, I broke up the ice on the main cistern each morning with a crowbar.

I saw it as part of the path of rebuilding my life after the accidents to finish and restore the beautiful, hand-built house with hand-plastered walls and hand-oiled barn-wood floors, multiple woodstoves, and deep-pocketed windowsills for sitting in luminous New Mexico morning light drinking piñon coffee. The house did not have an indoor toilet but I built a washroom with a Mexican Talavera tile sink, a rock-lined shower, and an antique claw-foot bathtub. I had unearthed the old tub from the long-neglected garden, where it was covered beyond obscurity in brambles of thorny desert weeds. I restored the finish and brought it inside, and it symbolized for me all that I loved about the house and the irony and deliciousness of building it. Building a temple in the middle of the harshest land I had ever been on, I saw it as a metaphor for all I was going through: rugged, unlikely, isolated, and somewhere inside of it all, a direly beautiful process. The house was feminine, like the exposed red earth landscape. It was improbable, like my own healing at that time—living on rainwater? In the desert? Building a house while you're still in recovery? Yes and yes and yes...

{2}

One winter night, a worker who I had hired to help with some finish plaster stayed too late. It was a bitter cold desert night, below zero, and the woodstoves were churning logs to ash nearly as fast as I could feed them in. I had been pushing myself too hard, and it was too cold. My neck seethed with pain as I helped the plasterer clean up his tools.

Remember, the house was miles from the nearest neighbor, over 30 miles from town. I closed the door and said goodbye and walked into the kitchen to get a beer. When I came back down the steps into the living room the worker was standing there inside. "I want to connect with you," he said. "I feel that you're special." He took a step toward me. I asked him to please leave and he said, "Not yet." I moved for the door and he blocked it. When he reached and touched my hand I went ballistic, I screamed a powerful and rage-filled litany of all that I had been through—being hit, the endless pain that doctors have no answers for, the chaos in my mind, my life's plan in shambles...

When I locked the door behind him after he left, I sat shaking on the rug in front of the woodstove, too upset to move. After the tears subsided I popped the now-warm beer that was sitting on the end table and attempted to answer the question of what the fuck I was doing out here in the middle of nowhere by myself building a house. "What exactly is it, Wren, you need to prove to yourself, anyway?"

It was a long night, and dawn found me still awake, curled in the bathtub, having made it through, once again.

{3}

Over the five years it took to finish the house, that bathtub was a place of exploration in the art of the sensuality of water. Cold white porcelain meets warmed nutrient-rich living rainwater, meets sun-parched, bone-dry skin. Alchemy occurs. I remember the days when I could only have three inches of water in my 'bath' that day, and other days when the cisterns were over-flowing and friends came over and we all took turns taking baths! And every day in between—reading books, shaving my sun-burned, wind-scorched legs, drinking wine, bathing while a friend or lover made food in the kitchen up the steps from the tub, soaking my seething neck muscles after a day wrestling straw bales into place on another section of the house...

I became an apprentice to the luxury of that one small bit of sacred water. It was never a given, always a Gift.

Chapter 2
THE NOISE INSIDE

I woke just after dawn, built and lit fires in the two woodstoves, gathered my things, and headed out across the sprawling sage-lands, down the plateau, to the place where hot lithium waters pour from the earth. As I dropped my body down into the minerally pool, the noise stopped.

I didn't realize, at first, that the 'noise' was even there. It had built up over time and took me a while to actually become aware of it. At first, I would hear the sharp sounds of the actual crash—the crunching of metal and the car roof dragging on asphalt—and it would wake me up at night. Later, every sound became too much—a blender, a hair dryer, music, people's voices. For a whole stretch of months, I barely left the house. My sweetie would leave for work and I spent day after day after day in complete silence. Even the noise of the first rush of water while running a bath shook my system. I don't think I understood then what was happening. I was enduring, working through, and untangling the noise inside. Over time, it got less dramatic and I could briefly go into public places, ride in cars (and eventually drive), talk on the phone, or listen to soothing music played quietly...

It wasn't until I sank down into one of the hot mineral pools one crystalline New Mexico morning—and heard the noise inside actually *stop*—that I fully realized that it was there.

Ahhhhhhhhhhh..... Wait, what's that?

Nothing.

Nothing!

How long had it been since I heard nothing? No doldrum beating (grief). No buzzing static (fear). No endless ringing (trauma). The water silenced the agony inside and, by giving me the gift of silence, I could see the tremendous dissonant symphony that had been existing in my head. It was a revelation.

After that I made my way the thirty miles down the plateau to the springs to soak at least three mornings a week for most of five years. More healing occurred in those waters than I will ever know. What I do know is that it's not true anymore what the doctors said: that I'll never work again, not be able to carry more than ten pounds, never live a 'normal' life. Anything I brought to the water—the grief, the rage, the incessant physical pain, the mental exhaustion of staying motivated to 'get through it,' the fatigue of my hope that it would all end—the water took and quelled and quieted. Every time, I emerged renewed, softened, different.

I would not have made it through the years it ended up taking to rebuild some semblance of that 'normal life' they were talking about without soaking. Disarming this noise inside was critical, like dismantling a smoke alarm going off in my brain! I still have too much static inside, more than I wish, and it is still to the waters I go to find my own silence inside the womb of water.

Chapter 3
ORIGINAL BLUEPRINT

{1}

The first 'healer' of any kind that I went to see was in a tucked away little office in downtown Santa Fe. The waiting room was ugly, full of closed brown doors. When Robert came to get me, we stepped through one of those brown doors into a whole different Universe. Three steps down into his sanctuary, the air was cool and everything was one shade or another of blue-grey. Perfectly framed artist renditions of sacred geometries graced the walls, and above the table upon which I would lie and begin our work together was a floating mobile, again a sacred geometrical pattern, which moved fluidly in the calm that enveloped the entire scene. A Journey has to begin somewhere and, so, here it began in Robert's office.

Robert practiced cranial sacral therapy, and I was drawn to seeing him because the friend who had recommended him had said, "It's basically like he barely touches you or moves you at all." *Great!* I thought, because that was about all I could handle at that moment—nothing. Lying on Robert's table with my eyes closed while he did his 'nothing' was truly stunning. He told me that the cellular structure of my body had an *original blueprint,* a memory of wholeness and organization that preceded the scrambled eggs I had become in the accident. And, he said, like a pile of iron filings strewn about, all it takes is a magnet to 'organize' them.

Robert was acting as that magnet as he held my body and allowed me to remember a pre-accident version of myself. I was cold and trepidatious at first, until I surrendered a bit, and then I noticed a calm, and again a kind of 'nothing' in the absence of agitation. "When you leave here," he would say, "go home and take a bath with plenty of salt. In the water your body can continue this work of remembering, and the salt transports information between your cells."

I saw Robert only a handful of times in those early weeks when even getting out of bed to go to his office was mostly more than I could manage in a day, and then one thing led to another and it was time for other healers, more steps along the journey. But I have never forgotten Robert's words, 'original blueprint,' and the ramification of following a path that would lead me home to that possibility...

{2}

Each person's original blueprint comes into being in water, in the amniotic fluid inside the womb. In water, then, we can undress to and realign with the deliciousness of our original design. As the clarity to build a bathhouse emerged, nearly a decade after my time on Robert's table, people would inquire where my determination to do such a lofty task came from, and the reply began to echo inside me. "I feel it is my 'sacred assignment,' the thing I can't help but do, the gift I have to give the world because of what I've been given," I said. Creating the capacity for people to access and realign with their more essential self feels like a mission I have been blessed to undertake.

Robert's words echo: "In water, your body can remember its *original blueprint.*" Healing occurs.

{3}

People don't have to *know* why their weekly trip to the pools transforms them. When Soak first opened, I was amazed that when people came out of their tub rooms, I literally would not recognize them as the same people who had gone in an hour before. The transformation was that visible. Through our daily lives, we carry around heavy and extensive baggage—roles, obligations, personas, pain, and a busyness that keeps us far away from our essential selves. When I drop my agenda and sink into the salty warm abyss of a tub, I always emerge a better person. I feel more like myself, more present. I don't always remember anymore that I am restoring myself in the most fundamental of ways to allow my body (and psyche) to remember its wholeness, but the beauty is that it happens anyway, whether I am conscious of it or not.

"The first ten minutes in a private tub I felt self-conscious," one man who had recently gone through a loss wrote to me. "What was I doing here? I should be cleaning or organizing or something... Then time shifted for me and I closed my eyes and allowed myself to float and be held in the warm waters in peace and the next thing I knew there was a gentle knock at the door saying my hour was up. Somehow, in that hour I transcended time and space and left feeling in touch with my own ability to find peace and gratitude and pleasure amidst the chaos of life. Thank you, Soak."

Part II
{Destress}

Chapter 4
UNDRESS

{1}

"What's your fifty-thousand-dollar problem?" a consultant once asked me. "Meaning, if I told you I could cure it on the spot, what would you pay me $50,000 for?"

The answer came instantaneously: *to never worry about my weight again.*

The vanity and seeming inconsequentiality of this reply is embarrassing. A friend is dying of cancer. Many are single mothers struggling to pay their bills. One lost a child. And I don't want to worry about my weight?

When we moved from rural Massachusetts to chic Southern California, I was a chunky twelve-year-old who hadn't lost my baby fat yet. The climate was vicious, as popularity was based primarily on thinness and everyone else was ridiculed or ignored. I wracked myself with dieting, obsessively exercised on the Stairmaster I moved into my bedroom, and eventually became what some would call anorexic, heading off to college weighing 103.

Escaping Southern California for the redwoods and real people up North, I quickly fell into a group of forest-activist hippie friends who ate tofu and smoked pot, loved to hike, had intelligent conversations, and—wait for it—were not obsessed with being thin! I think I knew people like that existed, but I had never met any of them. Healing began.

Later on, as a writing student in graduate school, I wrote a monthly column for a Los Angeles publication called *Vision Magazine*. One month I challenged myself to get honest about the underbelly of my struggles with weight. A line from that article still sits with me to this day. "To know that someone will read these words is to admit that I have drunk the poison of a culture that loves to be thin," I wrote. "And it has made me sick, very sick." The letters poured in. Hundreds of women commented, sharing their own stories and thanking me for speaking openly about a topic that affected their own lives so deeply, yet one they were mostly too ashamed to admit or talk about. The editor said it was the most commented-on article in the history of the magazine. One person willing to say, "I struggle," gave permission to so many others to do the same. It was a beautiful experience.

{2}

And here's where my love affair with water comes in: Water requires that we undress, that we disrobe from the hiding and protection of clothing. When faced with the conundrum to stay hidden or to get wet, for me, water always wins.

Throughout the world, bathing is considered a spiritual necessity. In many cultures, undressing and entering into any manner of water or sauna is as common as shopping or Happy Hour is in this country. Naked bathing rituals are done single-gender and co-ed, daily and for celebrations, and in every season of the year.

In Japan, public bathing is an unquestioned way of life, a poignant part of the longevity of the people in their culture. For the Finns, bathing is considered holy, a spiritual necessity. Women give birth in saunas, which they call a 'bath' because it is considered the cleanest place in the house, and the parliament buildings all have their own saunas where it is common for important meetings and discussions to be held—yes—naked.

Here in North America, public bathing is admittedly more fringe. Enthusiasts of hot springs are known to hike many miles just to partake in a rumored pool on the edge of a wilderness river, or plan whole road trips seeking the next springs. I know because I've lived my whole adult life this way—sometimes driving literally hours out of the way to investigate hot water, even when a trip had a tight timeframe. There is no counting the miles I have hiked, sometimes to discover just a stinking bog full of slime, or to be rewarded with the most majestic, pristine, rock-lined pool perched on a mountainside. And in these places, both remote and roadside, I have met the most eclectic people, people who shared stories about every other hot spring and bathhouse they have explored, people of every age and disposition, body-type and economic class, people whose bliss is in direct proportion to being in water. These are my people.

Now, I swim in every wild river, creek, stream, pond, or lake that I can get myself into. Clandestine roadside undressing, tiptoeing through poison oak to reach the banks, arduous hikes to reach mountain lakes cold as marble, all forms of trespassing, waking before it's humanly acceptable to be in the water as the first sun touches the rippling surface...and in every season. At this point countless strangers and acquaintances have seen me naked, and I highly doubt I have a single friend I haven't undressed in front of.

{3}

"First, I thought I'd never come here because I am too shy about my body," a woman recently said to me at Soak. "Then I thought I would only go in a private tub room. After that I thought, okay, the community tub, but only with a bathing suit. Now I bathe here weekly, naked, and have relaxed into myself in ways I never could have imagined."

The experience at Soak of another woman, Karin, has touched me deeply. She's one of those people you like immediately when you meet them. She's warm, inviting, and pretty. When Karin first came to Soak, she brought her friend Tamara, both large woman with chronic pain issues, and they each wanted a private tub to themselves. Friends often soak together, but I thought I understood why this might be a stretch for them.

After a couple of visits, Karin started sharing her story with me. She said she'd gained a tremendous amount of weight because her husband had encouraged her to eat whatever she wished, and she had become frustrated and embarrassed. Unable to really 'fit' in her conventional bathtub at home, she could never fully float, escape, or get the weight off of her joints. At Soak, she found the room to unwind, let go, and be held by the water.

As she and Tamara began to come more regularly, they both said their chronic pain significantly lessened, and they began to share a tub. I can only guess at the healing that occurred as they undressed to themselves and allowed the shapes of their bodies to be seen, accepted, and indulged. This is the Medicine of being 'allowed' to undress.

Seeing women and men of all body types together in a non-judgmental environment engaging in the healing art of bathing is the remedy to that poison I wrote about having drunk so many years ago. We've been infected by isolated images of 'perfect' bodies in the media, but we can heal from the self-loathing about our bodies that is a rampant and cancerous part of our society by seeing 'real people's bodies' in bathhouses, public pools, or community river spots. Admittedly, my mind still dabbles far too often in the dark art of judging the quality of my life by the way my favorite pair of jeans fits. However, more than a decade after writing that article, I have the honor of priestessing a space where I and others can engage with and unwind the negative stories we carry about our bodies.

An older man who became a regular opened up to me one afternoon, telling me that finding Soak pulled him out of a long-term depression, that he has lost fifteen pounds, feels better in his body than he has in years, and has found the spark to live again.

Water transforms all that it touches. It wears away stone, carves whole valleys, and turns the entire planet green. I will continue to let it transform me, as well, one quick skinny dip or one good long soak at a time...

Chapter 5
WATER AS WITNESS

{1}

"When it's over, I want to say: all my life I was a bride married to amazement."
– Mary Oliver

In Spring on the Oregon Coast, a violent wind blows north. Many days going for a walk on the beach entails leaning forward into a wind so fierce you can hardly make progress. This was one of those days. We met in an empty parking lot, he in our old white Toyota truck and me in my blue Subaru—another set of things we had recently split. Our visit to the sea on this day had a purpose: It was our 'unwedding' day.

A friend had introduced us on a warm Spring day, eight years prior, on a farm in Southern Oregon, and the spark of recognition was immediate. "Would you like to take a walk around the land?" he asked. When we got to the lower pond, we just looked at each other and, without a word, undressed.

A lovership begun in water, now ending in water. We had met this blustery morning to throw our rings into the sea. "There is nothing else big enough," I had said to him, "to hold my grief at this moment."

We pushed our way through the searing wind wordlessly. We had no script to follow. I was weeping hard, but the wind was taking the tears as soon as they left the corners of my eyes and replacing them with a ubiquitous layer of fine sand across my face. The wind was so loud we couldn't have heard each other even if there had been something to say.

In a deeply receded low tide, we walked the damp sand to the water's edge, slowly. This was it—the lapping sea and the salt of our tears. Without premeditation, I said, "Let's tell each other what we are unmarrying!" And so the final words we ever spoke in our relationship ensued. "I let go of all that doesn't work between us, all the fighting (I'll never throw a chair at you again!), the judgements, the stuckness, and the ways we keep each other small." "I unmarry our bad habits, our drinking, and all the things I can't stand about you—your indecisiveness. I unmarry your indecisiveness!"

...And with our lists completed, we took off our rings. He retrieved a thread of seaweed from the damp sand, tied the rings together, and we hurled them into the cold and steely-gray fathomless rolling ocean.

Like standing in front of a priest in order to 'sanctify' something, the water was our witness that day, the officiate of the ceremony. I needed a force larger than myself to midwife that moment, proving again that, in water, moments that can seem unsurvivable, can be endured.

{2}

And water, too, gives us a substance within which to reconnect...

Some beloved friends of mine went through a rough spell in their long marriage. One left when she just couldn't see the way through. The other held strong, waited, visualized her return. Both rallied much support from their community. You would see them with a friend on a bench, sidewalk, or beach, having a long teary hug or deep conversation. And then something gave way—the veil that had come in between them lifted just enough to find their way into a conversation. And this is where water comes in. They came to Soak to navigate these first tender explorations. At first they would meet in the community tub, to be together in a public space—safe, exploring the nearness of each other once again, the water as the medium to hold their negotiations.

As this occurred, I was reminded of a simple practice I was taught to employ during difficult conversations: *Place a bowl of water between the two people in conflict. As they speak, the water will absorb all of the negative or difficult charge and resolution is much more likely. Then, after the conversation, pour the water onto the earth...*

My friends were employing this simple, shamanic practice in a much larger sense—having the tough conversations *in* the water! I remember at least three potent meetings they had at Soak. Naked talks submersed in the big, salty tub with morning light pouring in, wrapping in towels to retreat to the cooling deck and lean on the railings overlooking the boatyard as the conversations continued, then back to the tub, and so on...tears, hugs, moments of stuckness, staying with it. It was an honor to witness this medicine occurring. Eventually, a private tub suited them just fine. They got back together.

{3}

Water can hold emotions bigger than our own, midwife difficult transformations, usher in deep change, heal something we fear might be irreparably broken or impossible to accomplish. Things as tender and important as a true walking away—or a coming back together...

Chapter 6
GRIEF AND THE SEA

{1}

"The cure for anything is salt water: sweat, tears, or the sea."
–Isak Dinesen

I'd open my eyes and there it would be: day. My love still gone, my purpose unknown, somewhere in the middle of an endless healing journey. I would quickly dress and head to the water. On the beach by sunrise, I'd watch the tides and seals and wet sands making infinite, shifting patterns as they interplayed with crashing waters and winds. By the time my morning walk was complete I would have the strength to face my empty apartment again, to work for a few hours, before heading out to spend the afternoon trolling some remote shore or tidal marsh, looking in every contour of wind-eroded rock or sculpted driftwood or foaming breakwater for some answer to the indecipherable riddle of my broken world.

And I did see answers in that salty universe. I would sit quietly in the sand as sanderlings gathered to play their incessant game of tag with the tide-line, running out like little filings chasing a magnet when a wave retreated, plundering the sand crabs that bubbled up as the waters passed, then scrambling away in collective retreat with the next wave. I saw in them one piece of the story of what was missing in my life: community. And then I saw the rocks, like gods rising from the turbulent waters, enduring every storm unaltered, holding time, something unchanging, the home of nesting colonies of fragile bird species, untouched by man. In them I saw patience and strength. In an erotic tangle of kelp washed ashore I saw the dance of lovers, partnership. And in the seals' soft fat shiny bodies draped on island rocks in the sun, ease. In skies that were clear when I left the house, becoming ominous as the rain began to pock the beach sand, acceptance of change. Depression couldn't hold up against the weight of the beauty of all this water, and I shuddered with gratitude for the mysterious calling that had obsessed my mind with coming to the sea to heal.

Sanderling track drawing from beach journal

{2}

The day Molly rode up on her horse I was absorbed in the all-consuming daily task of tending to my grieving heart, sitting on the cliff overlooking the ocean where enormous rocks jutted from the waves a few hundred yards off shore. People don't just ride around on horses anymore, except, of course, when they do. And that day it took something as dramatic as a beautiful woman emerging like an apparition from the mist, bareback on her horse, to shake me from my self-involved revelries. She stopped beside me.

"Hello," I must have said.

"Hi."

She was a slight woman in her forties wearing a black leather vest. She had dark hair and perhaps the smell of liquor on her breath. I liked her immediately.

"Gorgeous day out here."

"Yeah."

"Do you ride your horse out here often?" I asked.

"No," she said. "This is Ginger. He's a good old boy, my daughter's horse. She's leaving for college this week. I'm a single mom and it's been just me and her for eighteen years. Ginger and I just needed a good long walk today."

Maybe I told her about my accidents, talked about healing, and maybe even about a broken heart and the mending power of the sea. And in another moment of miracle, she asked me if I wanted to ride Ginger. At certain points along the healing journey every task is monumental—getting out of your pajamas, leaving the house, riding in a car, taking a walk, grocery shopping, going to clean out your desk in the place you'll never be employed again, driving a car, being present enough to support a friend or partner, going for your first run, admitting despair. I had hurdled years of tiny victories and painful failures in these everyday steps of rebuilding. Molly's horse was another step. Enormous and gentle-mannered, he wore only a sheepskin saddle pad. The last horse I had ridden, many years ago in Santa Fe, had also been bareback. Then, now, all the in-between—my world felt like it was being woven back together by some invisible force holding the strings. I wrote in my journal that night: *This was not a dream, but it could have been.*

~

When the heart is breaking, sometimes only the sea is a salve big enough to assuage the waves of pain. When nothing makes sense, perhaps the crashing pounding endlessly shifting violent balm of torrid water all around is an echo that can calm the inner storm. I don't know. I never really knew why. I just knew that in that water I saw something more vast than my tears alone, something more endless than my pain, a cold deadly unfathomable place, and the wellspring of all life.

{3}

Ocean. Ocean. Ocean. I have come to be kissed and to learn how to kiss, that this rhythm may enter me like the long, drawn-out way two tongues learn the contours of each other, slowly. Sea, you have access to my privacy, and I want to know your language—tides and foghorn, ships going by. Is there anything more perpetual than the sea? The actual musculature enclosing the heart opens as I lay myself in the sea. Given buoyancy, the head drops back, the shoulders roll down, and the chest arcs open. Grief, therefore, has less place to hide in water.

{4}

I was spending two afternoons a week giving homeschool lessons to an exceptionally bright eight-year-old girl whose family I had met when I came to this remote beach town to heal and regroup. Sasha and I would traverse jungles of Oregon grape and coastal cedars to access remote hidden marshes and tide-lands, where we watched birds' intricate feeding patterns and plumages turning vibrant for the spring. We would frequent every high vista, scoping for the far-off spoutings of migrating grey whales and learning about weather and different types of clouds. Mentoring Sasha was part of what put me back together in that fragile time. Her curiosity was endless, and her creativity even more prolific. She was famous for saying things like: "Wait, wait! I have a poem!" and out would pour:

Time.
Plovers move as one.
The sonar of whales moving north, ancient conversation.

On one particular day, Sasha said she wanted to see the paintings of a semi-famous artist who had died a few years prior. His widow lived in a wind-blown hovel, literally on the beach sand, and naively we went to tap on her door to say hello. Annie answered, not overly surprised to see us. She was a nothing of a woman with kind but yellowing vacant eyes.

"Oh, course," she said. "Frank is all I think about. Let me show you his studio."

No one had cleaned a single centimeter of her house in years, or longer. Sand blew through the threadbare siding of Frank's studio. A paintbrush sat on the table.

"Don't touch that Sasha," Annie said. "That's where Frank left it when he put his brush down for the last time."

I don't know what I thought we were getting into that afternoon, but this wasn't it. Annie led us upstairs, past a room she called the 'kitchen'—just a liquor cabinet with some rotting food on the countertop. Reaching for a plastic gallon jug of vodka, Annie half-filled a glass, added a splash of juice, and asked us if we cared to join her. It wasn't yet noon and Sasha was eight. We all proceeded upstairs.

I hugged Sasha into me as I realized we hadn't come to Annie's to look at paintings, we had come to have a homeschool lesson about grief.

Some people give up, let the wind come inside, stop fighting against the inevitable entropy of a heart and a life. I saw myself in her. Me, a young, vibrant woman, her an old, delirious woman—both facing the same question: *How do you live with a broken heart?* Her answer was to leave everything exactly the way it was and wish forever that he wasn't gone. My answer was to feel everything all the way down through, until I was done feeling it, and from that bedrock, re-build.

Leaving Annie's, Sasha and I were quiet as we walked the tides. After a while, she spoke. "Wren," she said, "Why did you come here? I mean, you have no family here, no boyfriend."

"Sasha," I replied after a moment of pause, "I am like Annie in some ways. The things I have lost are haunting me. No eight-year old should *really* understand grief, but you will someday. It can make you look like a crazy woman, or someone whose life doesn't make any sense."

A juvenile bald eagle, with mottled brown plumage and a wingspan longer than either of us were tall, dove for a fish just off-shore at that moment, caught it, shook its wings above the water, and flew off.

"You know when we watch the big storms churn and roil and froth the sea into a rage?" I asked. "Or run to the cliffs to be there right at the exact moment the full moon emerges over perfectly flat evening water?"

"Yes," she said.

"I am letting the beauty here put me back together."

"What about Annie?" Sasha asked.

"Well, Sweetie, she's doing the opposite," I said. "She's letting the wind and the sea and the rain wash through her, hoping they will bring her to Frank more quickly."

"I see," she said. "Can we go home now?"

Part III
{Refresh}

Chapter 7

UNDIAGNOSIS

{1}

On my thirty-second birthday, I adopted a six-month-old German shepherd who had been found running along the highway in the scorching July heat. The searing asphalt had burned through all of her tough black paw pads to the tender pink skin inside. The Humane Society nursed her partially back to health before I came to retrieve her. We were both wary—I, *decidedly* not a dog person though I had gotten an itch to have a dog, and her, with an unknown story of abuse and a mysterious ordeal in order to escape, already in the history of her short life.

The temperature was over one hundred degrees the day I went to retrieve Dahlia. We had a two-hour drive back to our farm, and the air conditioner on max barely made a dent. Once we turned off the highway and onto the state route that snaked along the river, we bee-lined for a dusty lot near a waterhole.

Having no rapport with Dahlia yet, I didn't know what to expect as I put her on a leash and tentatively got her out of the car. She looked at me, glanced around, saw the water, and bolted. Leash flying, she was in the river prancing and splashing before I even knew what had happened. I joined her. We swam and splashed and hugged, no leash required (basically ever again for that matter). This was *my* dog!

Nursing Dahlia's feet back to full health and bringing her into her new life at the farm was a beautiful process of witnessing restoration. One of my favorite of her idiosyncrasies is that, when I put a bowl of water down for her, the first thing she does is put her front paws in it, standing in the bowl. Only after she's done her 'dip', she'll drink.

Dahlia came with me everywhere. Because of her fantastic nature she could wait outside of shops or restaurants and greet passersby anytime I needed her to. Entertainingly, she'd sit in the back of the truck and watch people, or if I was on a longer errand she'd sleep curled like a coyote for hours without complaint.

Then, one day, I was vending my handmade jewelry at a craft fair and met Pamela, a fellow artisan who had her dog *with her* at her booth—while mine was outside in the truck. "Jackson is a service dog," she said. "He helps me with my anxiety. Legally, he can go with me anywhere."

Wait a minute… Dahlia was *my* service dog! I called around. "You need a medical diagnosis," I was told. "You could easily be diagnosed with PTSD from your accidents." I hung up. Dahlia and I went to the river to think.

I never wanted to say the acronym 'PTSD' and my name in the same sentence. Once the mind believes it "has" something, it starts to convince the body. I knew I was traumatized, shattered, and upended, and that my life was a reflection of this turmoil in many more ways than I wanted to admit. I had a noise inside I could not quiet. But I did not think I "had" PTSD.

Dahlia's paws don't hurt anymore, but she still dips them in water every chance she gets, like when she's found standing in a stranger's dog bowl or fountain. And though my injuries have subsided, I am still leery of crowds, noise, stress, travel, bright lights… Trauma lingers. I skipped the diagnosis and opted for taking Dahlia with me everywhere we'd rather be anyway—the beaches, rivers, and mountain lakes that quiet my rattled self back to stillness.

{2}

PTSD can loosely be defined as a cycle of symptoms that deliver continuous and uninterrupted sources of suffering. The U.S. military has initiated a rehabilitation program on California beaches utilizing surfing to annul the life-ravaging effects of PTSD in young vets coming back from the Middle East. "In combat, we wait and wait, then fire and attack," one soldier explained. "In surfing, you wait and wait, and then have an adrenaline and endorphin rush of beauty instead." Aptly named, *Ocean Therapy* is having profound results.

After surf sessions the soldiers sit on the sand, talking and laughing. "They never do that," a supervisor for the program noted. "They don't talk to each other. They don't laugh." Water is known to assuage trauma and, now, through the data collected in programs such as Ocean Therapy, research is proving that regular surfing sessions (or it is just being out in the ocean?) disrupts the cycle of suffering and rebalances brain chemistry.

It is known that when submerged in water, our bodies alter the balance of epinephrine and dopamine to the levels achieved during meditation. One vet, who admitted he had made the decision to kill himself before his friend drug him to a surfing session, is now an instructor in the program. "Guys are heading back every day, indescribably damaged," he said. "I know because I've been there. I want to get them out of the bar and off of the firing range, and into the ocean."

Where can a person who has been shot at, who has shot at others, who has witnessed scenes and survived experiences more gruesome and inhumane than anyone should ever have to see or endure, go to recover?

Water Prayer. Holy Ocean. Blessed Reset Button. Always there, lapping on the sand, ready to give its watery Gift.

{3}

When Soak first opened, there was a veteran who used to come in regularly. It always struck me as a beautiful thing that this strong hulk of a man would take the time get in a private tub for an hour to unwind, that he saw the value that tending to himself in this way was creating in his ongoing recovery. Eventually, he started telling me stories of being in Iraq. Sometimes, after he left, I would just sit behind the desk and weep.

This is what I built this bathhouse for. For you. For me. Because too many of us have endured too much. Because I believe healing can and does occur. I see it every day.

This is how Soak's tagline was born—Undress. Destress. Refresh.

Chapter 8
ANGELS

{1}

In the brief second before the car flipped after being hit, I literally heard a voice that said, "Just hold on, you will be okay, but this is something you have to go through." I actually saw in my mind's eye the car being 'held' as it tumbled and landed upside down in the ditch against the mountainside.

{2}

Within that first post-accident week a woman named Rowena who was a loose acquaintance of my partner at the time, Greg, heard about what had happened and contacted him to let us know she would like to help. "Sure," Greg had said on the phone, "What do you have in mind, would you like to bring us some food or something?"

"No," Rowena said. "I want to help with Wren's healing. There are some incredible alternative practitioners in this town, and I want her to be able to go and see them. Don't worry about the money."

A silence fell as Greg digested what he was hearing. This woman had never met me, and very loosely even knew Greg. "I just have a feeling I need to support her," she had said, adding, "Please, here are some people I recommend when she is ready..."

The journey that ensued between Rowena and I lasted eight years. Healer after healer she led me to unwound my trauma and rewove me back together. Unquantifiable amounts of money were spent. She insisted. At one time we traveled to a specialty clinic on the East Coast together (a trip alone that almost killed me at that point because I was barely able to leave the house, let alone fly across the country), where a team of specialists worked on me for eight continuous hours a day for a week.

Rowena was in her sixties when we met. She had suffered greatly her whole life with a lung condition and associated complications that had led to a life of doctor's offices and healer's tables. Her main endeavor was surviving each day. The first thing Greg and I ever helped her with was selling the beautiful adobe house she had just bought in Santa Fe only to find out she couldn't move in because the VOC's of all the new building materials were making her violently ill. Over time, we became her self-elected personal assistants because the logistics of life so deeply overwhelmed her. The three of us became the profoundest and most unlikely of friends.

Rowena had more money than god, it turned out, and she would choose people who 'came to her' and support them with any manner of healing they needed. Because of all she had been through, she felt it was her mission. Among other things, I watched her support a drug-addicted teen and his mother, who was wracked with fibromyalgia, donate all of the funds needed to build a schoolhouse 'temple' building for a prominent shaman she adored, and pay the rent for her favorite T'ai Chi teacher for years on end so he could give his gift to the world.

{3}

On one of the last mornings I ever saw Rowena, we were in Brazil. A group of us gathered to hike to a sacred site in the tropical morning as the long-tailed hummingbirds and tropical warblers sang the forest awake. The long damp path descended into a canyon where, at the trail's end, a sacred waterfall was used for the explicit purposes of healing and rejuvenation. Access to the fall was completely private, and only granted to those who had been "prescribed" to go to the spring by the famous healer we had traveled to Brazil to see.

Rowena had trepidations about the hike, as her failing lungs and compromised body weren't really up for the task. I hooked my arm through hers and we walked down the trail at the speed of a toddler, in awe of the gift of visiting this place and receiving whatever blessing the water had in store.

As we reached the final descent, the group of us gathered together in a circle and we each said a few words of prayer about what we were ready to let go of—a woman at the end of her journey with cancer, a man whose broken heart was longing to be healed, others with ancestral grief, or psychological pain, a beautiful woman whose body was riddled with MS, Rowena's sixty-year journey of being sick, my accidents... There was profuse weeping, we sang an ancient blessing song for healing, and then the rest of the experience was had in silence. One by one, we were guided to hold a bar that had been drilled into the rock behind the falls to steady ourselves against the intensity of the torrent of falling water. And then we entered.

Time stopped. The water had no temperature. The pummeling was not unpleasant. In the deafening rush of pounding water, a veil of utter silence fell. It was only when the guide reached in to touch my hand and retrieve me that I had any concept of how long it had been. I felt a sense of never wanting to leave, similar to people who talk about near-death experiences, where an angelic, all-pervasive light is irresistibly and indescribably compelling.

My time was up. I watched Rowena receive her water blessing and helped her back to the path. As radiant as I had ever seen her, she actually looked like a child. We all walked the long trail back in silence, shimmering.

{4}

When word came that Rowena had passed peacefully in her room one morning, not a mile from the falls we had visited together a few months prior, I wept and wept. Her wild, cherubic, childlike face dripping with water—renewed, ready to be done enduring all the pain she had in this life—flashed in front of my eyes.

Thank you, thank you, Angels.

Chapter 9
COURTED BY THE SEA

{1}

In many ways it began in water.

I met him in a dark driveway in a winter rain. Looking up at the dripping boughs of towering cedars, I said, "It must take some getting used to, this rain."

"I don't know, he said, "It just sort of feels like a long sweet kiss to me."

"Wow," I said, a little shocked by his response and somewhat terrified of how my heart and spirit might shut down living in the cold wet place I had just moved to. "How long have you been here?"

"Twenty years."

"Do you ever think about leaving?"

"Not really."

An energy between us made the conversation notably awkward. I could have stood there in the dark drizzle for a long time but, of course, that was ridiculous. We were at his ex-wife's house, for one thing, and he had friends inside waiting for him to come back in and retrieve them for a ride home. We said a few more clumsy words before I scrambled to my car.

The next time we saw each other was months later, when a text came through about meeting at the water's edge to dip in the Sound with some mutual friends. And so it began in earnest—a courtship in and by the water. After that, many mornings found me quickly bundling up in a pile of layers, gathering supplies, and hurrying to the water to be there at dawn with him and others. We began a ritual of morning swims, sometimes with ensuing fires, thermoses of hot cacao elixirs, sage to burn, prayers, naked running down the beach, sacred silence, or playful shenanigans, depending on the day.

By late Spring our meetings at the water also included afternoon walks, long conversations lying in the sand, picnic dinners on the beach, evening swims, and once a late-night impromptu dip when the phosphorescence was in bloom and the skin on our whole bodies danced with light as we splashed and played in the moonless flat black water.

So maybe it wasn't a surprise that he wanted to meet at the water one afternoon when he called to let me know he had something to tell me.

"We've been getting really close lately," he said. "And I need to tell you that I have been seeing someone else."

"What?"

"She lives in another town, and I'm leaving in the morning to go see her for the weekend."

Tears that I had wished weren't there began to blur the long delicious view of open water across the Sound. And then a conversation occurred about healing and dating and being ready and not trusting women (or was it himself?) after the dissolution of a marriage...

...and, there, with the sky and the earth as our witness, I did what in the past for me would have been unthinkable: I understood. "I get it," I said. And much to both of our surprises, I added, "I'm not going anywhere."

I cried on and off all that night. We had been courting for months and my heart had deeply opened to him. By dawn though, I was clear what needed to be done.

I recalled a story that a magical and wise friend of mine

had told me. When she met the man who is now her husband, they courted and, in time, he told her he was seeing someone else, and that he needed to go and visit this other woman and feel what was there between them in light of this new connection with my friend. She went to work with her prayers and feminine magic, and sent him off with all her blessings and a little medicine pouch she had made for him. "I knew he would come back to me," she had said. "And I knew he needed to go there to find that out. So I trusted, and gave him the space to have his own discovery about the power of our connection."

That morning, I filled my giant bathtub with herbs and salts and oils and I brewed a prayer for our budding love and for the protection of my own heart. And, soaking that all in, I let go.

From the tub, wanting to transmit something of that prayer to him to take on his trip to see her, I sent these words:

As the water licks the sand, that slow continuous conversation, I await our unfolding connection, fluid as waves. As this morning's tide washes away the evidence of our feet in last night's sand, all things are renewed, kissed, blessed. Enjoy.

{2}

He was on the ferry home a few days later when I got the message back. "I'm home," it read. "Meet me at the water."

CODA

These days, I am having an affair with Soak. I wake before the rest of the town, unlock the big knotty alder door with the seahorse door handle, enter the dark bathhouse, and undress. I fire up the sauna, slip into a tub, walk around naked in the lobby. Or I come in late at night and hose everything down, open everything up, play loud music, dance freely. I come in tired and in tears. I sit on the floor and pray. I ask the Spirit of Soak for her help, and I feed Her with flowers, incense, the smoke of cedar, a bowl of water with fresh petals floating, bells. And I come in when no one is around and play my cedar flute, ancient melodies filling every corner, blessing the waters, resonating and echoing and building beauty into the walls and architecture, tending the Wild Heart of the space itself. For all that Soak gives to others, for all She holds, for the medicine that this project is for me, I give back to her in these simple, sensuous ways—clandestine lovemaking, the affair of my heart.

SOAK IS OFFERING THREE WAYS TO ENGAGE

{1}
Become a Sister Site and bring the gift of Soak to your town!

{2}
Consult with us about building your own version of a bathhouse.

{3}
Leap your life's hurdles and manifest your dreams! Become a member of Wren's private coaching practice and find the YES to take your life's next steps.

To begin a conversation about any of the above, write to:
soakonthesound@gmail.com